Androcles
and the Lion

Retold by Jenny Alexander
Illustrated by Mark Peppé
Series Editor: Rosalind Kerven

Introduction

The story of Androcles and the Lion comes
from Ancient Rome.
The Roman army took over many countries
and made them part of the Roman Empire.
The Romans built great cities and roads.
They were clever engineers and craft-workers.

Map showing Ancient Rome

THE ROMAN EMPIRE

AFRICA

Rome

NORTH AFRICA

Mediterranean
Sea

Slaves of the Romans

The Romans took
many prisoners
of war.
They were taken
back to Rome
as slaves.
Rich households
had slaves to do
all the work, like
Junius, the boy in
this picture.

The Arena

The Romans enjoyed bloodthirsty entertainments.
They built arenas where trained fighters,
called gladiators, fought against each other,
or against wild animals.

This picture of a gladiator fighting a lion was painted on a wall.

Androcles was a slave.
From the moment he woke up in the morning
to the moment he went to bed at night,
he was forced to work.

His master was a rich but cruel man.
No matter how hard his slaves worked,
he always found a reason to beat them.
Androcles longed to run away.
But he knew that if he was caught
trying to escape, he would be killed.

One day his master
took Androcles on a journey to Africa
to buy olive oil and purple dyes.
They sailed in a big cargo ship.
A group of animal-catchers travelled with them.
Their cages stood ready for the fierce wild
animals they would bring back.

When they arrived in Africa, Androcles was excited
by the wonderful sights and smells that greeted him.
That night he lay awake, wishing he was free.
Here, so far from Rome, anything seemed possible,
even freedom.
He got up and slipped silently out of the camp.

Then he ran.
The ground was rough,
with no path to guide him.
He had only the stars to light his way.
Sometimes he slowed down, exhausted;
but then he thought he heard soldiers chasing him
and he forced himself to go on.

Soon the lights of the camp were just pinpricks
in the blackness and the night closed around him,
like a thick, heavy blanket.
His legs were trembling with tiredness and fear
and his chest was beginning to ache.
He had to stop.

As he stood there struggling to catch his breath,
he heard a sound that made his blood run cold.
Something was breathing close behind him.
He heard a twig snap, and a low growl.
Androcles spun round.

There, right behind him, stood a huge lion!
The lion opened his mouth and roared.
Androcles almost fell over with fright.
He took a step backwards.
The lion roared again.
Androcles was too frightened to move.
The lion took a step towards him ...

But as the lion's front paw touched the ground
he gave a yelp of pain.
Androcles saw that the paw was red and swollen.
Androcles knew all about pain, for he had suffered
many beatings from his cruel master.
He felt sorry for the huge animal,
and his pity was stronger than his fear.

Slowly, he edged towards the lion, holding out his
hand in friendship.
He held his breath and lifted up the swollen paw.
He saw a long sharp thorn sticking into
the lion's soft flesh.

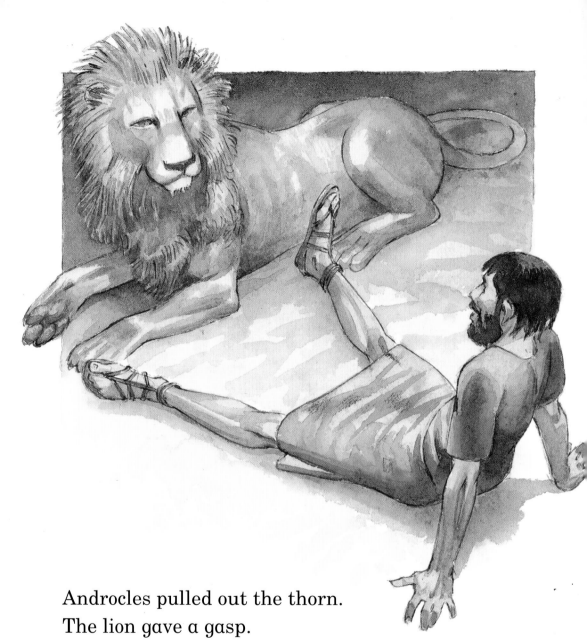

Androcles pulled out the thorn.
The lion gave a gasp.
Then he stood back on all fours and roared again
with relief and happiness.
He didn't try to eat Androcles.
Instead he lay down at his feet,
and when Androcles walked away,
the lion followed him.

Androcles felt safe with the lion to protect him.
They found a cave to live in.
Every day the lion went hunting and brought back
his catch to share with Androcles.
They lived that way for three years.

But Androcles missed other people, and he
missed Rome.
One day, when the lion was out hunting
he decided it was time to go home.
Surely no-one would recognize him, after so long?

Androcles was unlucky.

As soon as he got to Rome he bumped straight into his old master!

Androcles was arrested by soldiers and thrown into prison.

Some days later
they took him in chains to the arena
where prisoners were fed to the wild animals.
The crowds shrieked and yelled all around him,
hungry for his blood.
He saw the Emperor sitting among them.
The Emperor looked bored.

18

At the far side of the arena, the bars of the
animals' cages glinted in the scorching sun.
One of them was opening...

There was a mighty roar.
A massive lion came bursting out of the cage
and stood wild-eyed on the shimmering sand.

Androcles' legs gave way beneath him.
He dropped to his knees and hid his face in his hands.
He heard the lion pacing towards him...

But then nothing happened!
The crowd fell silent.
Slowly, Androcles dared to open his eyes.
The lion was sitting quietly in front of him.
Androcles was no longer frightened.
He took the lion's paw in his hands,
and saw the old scar from the thorn.

The crowd gave a whoop of delight.
This was something they had never seen before!
Even the Emperor stopped looking bored,
and stood up.
"Let the slave go free!" he shouted.
"What about the lion?" cried the people.
The Emperor said,
"Let the lion be his reward."

And so Androcles became a free man at last.
He and the lion went everywhere together
and wherever they went, people stopped to stare.
"There goes Androcles, who made friends with the
lion," they said to each other.
"And there goes the lion who remembered his friend."